500 CC
Computer Citations

500 CC
Computer Citations

Vincent F. Hendricks

ISBN 1-904-987-09-5
King's College Publications
Scientific Director: Dov Gabbay
Managing Director: Jane Spurr
Department of Computer Science
Strand, London WC2R 2LS, UK
kcp@dcs.kcl.ac.uk
www.dcs.kcl.ac.uk/kcl-publications/

Cover design by Richard Fraser, www.avalonarts.co.uk
Printed by Lightning Source, Milton Keynes, UK

To my sisters

Vianna and Zara Vang Olsen

Contents

Preface

Computers ... we all have some relation to computers. Either because we voluntarily choose to use them 24–7 – at home, at work, as a leisure activity in the park, in a restaurant – or because they involuntarily hold all our sensitive information. They also make sure that our tax-returns add up, that air- and space-travel is possible, that difficult weather predictions can be made enabling us to plan for the next skiing trip, and so forth. Computers are responsible for an ever growing number of operations in daily and scientific life. They have made things possible that could not have been imagined earlier, but they have also generated problems which were never dreamt of before they became the new life companions of modern man. *500 CC* records the experiences we have as computer users, abusers and Internet-cruisers—from rage and anger via joy, laughter and appreciation to despair and frustration.

In the computing community – especially among the professional computer scientists and programmers – there is a tacit understanding that much computer code is, or should be, freeware. All the material for this book has been compiled from the Internet and may be viewed as the source code of our experiences with computers. To honor this liberal understanding in the community *500 CC: Computer Citations* may be downloaded free of charge in PDF-format from $\frac{VINCE}{INC}$.com at

http://www.vince-inc.com/500CC.html

This book completes the trilogy of quotations. First came *Feisty Fragments: For Philosophy*, second *Logical Lyrics: From Philosophy to Poetics* and thirdly here is *500 CC: Computer Citations*. The three books are independent of one another, yet the triplet choice of themes is not arbitrary. Philosophy, logic and computers concern us all—and philosophy, logic and computers concern each other. Philosophy without logic is without guide, logic without philosophy is without content, logic and philosophy guide us guiding computers. There will be no such thing as artificial intelligence without intelligence, and no such thing as human intelligence without philosophical reflection and logical tools of mind. The trilogy is a humorous, inquisitive and critical witness to the relation between philosophy and its broader intellectual environment.

———————————— @ ————————————

I would like to acknowledge the global computing community which have provided citations and quotes to be found in *500 CC: Computer Citations*. This book is a tribute to all—professionals as well as laymen.

First and foremost I'm utterly indebted to Henriette Kibsgaard for thinking, enjoying, laughing, in short – being – with me.

I would like to extend my gratitude to Johan van Benthem, Kevin Warwick, John Symons, and Teit Molter for their continuous encouragement and support.

I would like to thank my proof-reader Henriette Holm and my New York City-mom Mimi Vang Olsen. My gratitude finally goes out to King's College Publications, in particular Scientific Director Prof. Dov M. Gabbay, Managing Director Jane Spurr, and Editorial Assistant Anna Maros for taking on the trilogy.

—Vincent F. Hendricks
July 2005
Copenhagen

Disclaimer

Material for *500 CC: Computer Citations* has exclusively been taken from the Internet—bulletin boards, usenet, quotation databases, discussion groups and listings, and miscellaneous webpages. Texts have sometimes been corrupt and references have mostly been missing. Full apologies are granted for any errors and omissions. If notified of any error or omission it will be rectified at the earliest opportunity. Copyright is not claimed and permissions have not been sought since the 'Fair Use'-law is assumed to apply—refer to page 157 for the Fair Use Statement.

Since no material has been included which is not to be found freely on the Internet, *500 CC: Computer Citations* may be downloaded freely in PDF-format from $\frac{\text{VINCE}}{\text{INC}}$.com at

http://www.vince-inc.com/500CC.html

—Vincent F. Hendricks
July 2005
Copenhagen

Jim Allchin

▶ *Microsoft group vice president / platforms product group*

I am a hard-core believer that the clean desktop is the way to go ... At the same time, we told OEMs that if they were going to put a bunch of icons on the desktop, then so were we.

Guy Almes

▶ *Chief engineer for Internet2*

There are three kinds of death in this world. There's heart death, there's brain death, and there's being off the network.

Stewart Alsop

▶ *General partner / NEA — New Enterprise Associates*

Gates is the ultimate programming machine. He believes everything can be defined, examined, reduced to essentials, and rearranged into a logical sequence that will achieve a particular goal.

Jeremy S. Anderson

▶ *American computer scientist*

There are two major products that came out of Berkeley: LSD and UNIX. We do not believe this to be a coincidence.

Mark Andreessen

▶ *Founder and chief operating officer, Netscape*

[The BLINK tag in HTML] was a joke, okay? If we thought it would actually be used, we wouldn't have written it!

† Anonymous

In the RoboCop film, the robot is running the MS-DOS COM-MAND.COM program.

Endless loop: See Loop, endless.

Lyall's Conjecture: If a computer cable has one end, then it has another.

Will the information super highway have any rest stops?

Difference between a virus and Windows? Viruses rarely fail.

Final definitive version: We can't stand looking at this any more.

The programmer awakes one day to find he has become the documentation he never wrote.

Computers are like air conditioners: They stop working when you open windows.

I had a fortune cookie the other day and it said: 'Outlook not so good'. I said: 'Sure, but Microsoft ships it anyway.'

Apparently, Windows98 is going to be renamed 'Diana, Princess of Windows'. It's overrated, overpriced, consumes loads of resources and crashes spectacularly ...

Programming is an art form that fights back.

People who think MS-DOS and Windows are the slickest thing since sliced butter should be forced to wear a sign stating 'This mind intentionally left blank'.

Any program will expand to fill all available memory.

Smith & Wesson—the original point and click interface.

I got bugs,
You got bugs,
All God's chilluns got bugs.

When I get to heaven,
Won't see no more bugs.

Why doesn't DOS ever say 'EXCELLENT command or file-name'?

Code's bug-free in God's heaven.

Remember when ... ? A computer was something on TV from a science-fiction show. A window was something you hated to clean and RAM was the cousin of a goat ... Meg was the name of my girlfriend and gig was your middle finger upright. Now they all mean different things and that really mega bytes. An application was for employment. A program was a TV show. A cursor used profanity. A keyboard was a piano. Memory was something that you lost with age. A CD was a bank account. And if you had a 3 1/2" floppy you hoped that nobody found out. Compress was something you did to the garbage not some-thing you did to a file. And if you unzipped anything in public you'd be in jail for awhile. Log on was adding wood to the fire. Hard drive was a long trip on the road. A mouse pad was where a mouse lived and a back-up happened to your commode. Cut you did with a pocket knife. Paste you did with glue. A web was a spider's home and a virus was the flu. I guess I'll stick to my pad and paper and the memory in my head. I hear nobody's been killed in a computer crash but when it happens they wish they were dead!

The most useless computer tasks are the most fun to do.

On a clear disk you can seek forever.

Artificial intelligence? No thank you, I don't need crutches.

Artificial Intelligence usually beats natural stupidity.

What does the Start button do—isn't the computer already running? —A Windows95 user.

There's always time to do it over and never time to do it right.

'Twas the night before crisis, and all through the house,
Not a program was working, not even a browse.

The programmers were wrung out, too mindless to care,
Knowing chances of cutover hadn't a prayer.

The users were nestled, all snug in their beds,
While visions of inquiries danced in their heads.

When out in the lobby, there arose such a clatter,
That I sprang from my tube to see what was the matter.

And what to my wondering eyes should appear,
But a Super Programmer, oblivious to fear.

More rapid than eagles, his programs they came,
And he whistled and shouted and called them by name.

On Update! On Add! On Inquiry! On Delete!
On Batch Jobs! On Closing! On Functions Complete!

His eyes were glazed over, his fingers were lean,
From weekends and nights in front of a screen.

A wink of his eye, and a twist of his head,
Soon gave me to know I had nothing to dread.

He spoke not a word, but went straight to his work,
Turning specs into code, then turned with a jerk.

And laying his finger on the ENTER key,
The system came up, and worked perfectly.

The updates, updated; the deletes, they deleted;
The inquires, inquired; and the closing completed.

He tested each whistle, he tested each bell,
With nary a crash, and all had gone well.

The system was finished, the tests were concluded,
The client's last changes were even included!

And the client exclaimed with a snarl and a taunt,
It's just what I asked for, but it's not what I want.

If you put a billion monkeys in front of a billion typewriters typing at random, they would reproduce the entire collected works of Usenet in about ... five minutes.

Want to make your computer go really fast? Throw it out the window!

Mac users swear by their Mac,
PC users swear at their PC.

Do bugs enjoy buggery as much as adults enjoy adultery?

People say Microsoft paid 14M$ for using the Rolling Stones song 'Start me up' in their commercials. This is wrong. Microsoft payed 14M$ only for a part of the song. For instance, they didn't use the line 'You'll make a grown man cry'.

$E = MC$ squared (Expectations = Machine Capacity Squared)

Real programmers don't comment code. If it was hard to write, it should be hard to understand!

Terminals are the suction cups of the information milking machine sucking on our knowledge nipples.

Real programmers don't write COBOL. COBOL is for wimpy application programmers.

To err is human. To really mess things up requires a computer.

You'll never really learn to swear until you get a computer.

Hardware: A product that if you play with it long enough, breaks.
Software: A product that if you play with it long enough, works.

Build a system that even a fool can use, and only a fool will use it.

If a program is useful, it must be changed.

If a program is useless, it must be documented.
If a program runs right, it must be obsolete.

Hardware: The parts of a computer system that can be kicked.

Never trust a computer you can't lift.

This program posts news to billions of machines throughout the galaxy. Your message will cost the net enough to bankrupt your entire planet. As a result your species will be sold into slavery. Be sure you know what you are doing. Are you absolutely sure you want to do this?

You know it is going to be a bad day when you forget your new password.

Computers have lots of memory but no imagination.

Those parts of the system that you can hit with a hammer (not advised) are called hardware; those program instructions that you can only curse at are called software.

The problem with troubleshooting is that trouble shoots back.

Real programmers never work from 9 to 5. If any real programmer is around at 9 a.m., it's because they were up all night.

If it draws blood, it's hardware.

I haven't lost my mind; I have a tape back-up somewhere.

Back up my hard drive? How do I put it in reverse?

RAM disk is not an installation procedure.

Give a person a fish and you feed them for a day; teach that person to use the Internet and they won't bother you for weeks.

The attention span of a computer is only as long as its power cord.

Making fun of AOL users is like making fun of the kid in the wheel chair.

Don't anthropomorphize computers—they hate it.

All programmers are playwrights and all computers are lousy actors.

Jesus saves! The rest of us better make back-ups.

In God we trust, all others we virus scan.

In a few minutes a computer can make a mistake so great that it would have taken many men many months to equal it.

Where a calculator on the ENIAC is equipped with 18,000 vacuum tubes and weighs 30 tons, computers in the future may have only 1,000 vaccuum tubes and perhaps weigh 1.5 tons.

It's not a bug—it's an undocumented feature.

If computers get too powerful, we can organize them into committees. That'll do them in.

I just wish my mouth had a backspace key.

True research is like fumbling in the dark for the right switches. Once you've turned the light on everyone can see ....

The C Programming Language: A language which combines the flexibility of assembly language with the power of assembly language.

Who is General Failure, and why is he reading my hard drive?

PASCAL: A programming language named after a man who would turn over in his grave if he knew about it.

The message 'Bad command or File Name' is about as informative as 'if you don't know why I'm mad at you, I'm certainly not going to tell you'!

CChheecckk yyoouurr dduupplleexx sswwiittcchh!

PCMCIA: People Can't Memorize Computer Industry Acronyms.

Windows, another fine product from the folks who gave us EDLIN.

If you don't double-click me, I can't do anything.

Men are from Mars. Women are from Venus. Computers are from hell.

Computers are not intelligent. They only think they are.

The Internet is mightier than the pen.

The sysadmin's motto: If it wasn't backed-up, then it wasn't important.

Do not meddle in the affairs of wizards, for they are subtle and quick to anger. Do not meddle in the affairs of dragons for you are crunchy and taste good with ketchup. Do not meddle in the affairs of cats, for they are subtle and will piss on your computer.

Go not to Usenet for counsel, for it will say both no, and yes, and no, and yes ...

Cardinal rule of computing: To go forward, you must back-up.

Guide to understanding a net.addict's day:

1. Slow day: didn't have much to do, so spent three hours on Usenet.

2. Busy day: managed to work in three hours of Usenet.

3. Bad day: barely squeezed in three hours of Usenet.

I'd love to change the world, but they won't give me the source code!

I just found out that the brain is like a computer. If that's true, then there really aren't any stupid people. Just people running DOS.

If you want to stop a computer from working you should use an OS-independent attack from an F-18. Such an attack can't be fixed by downloading a patch.

You make my software turn to hardware

Hackers do it with all sorts of characters.

Hackers do it with bugs.

Hackers do it with fewer instructions.

Hackers know all the right MOVs.

Hey! It compiles! Ship it!

Ooops. My brain just hit a bad sector.

Most of the VAX instructions are in microcode, but HALT and NO-OP are in hardware for efficiency.

Did anyone see my lost carrier?

Help! My keyboard is stuckkkkkkkkkkkkkkkk

586: The average IQ needed to understand a PC.

Computer programmers know how to use their hardware.

Like car accidents, most hardware problems are due to driver error.

Computers will not be perfected until they can compute how much more than the estimate the job will cost.

You can bring any calculator you like to the midterm, as long as it doesn't dim the lights when you turn it on.

Daddy, why doesn't this magnet pick up this floppy disk?

Daddy, what does FORMATTING DRIVE C mean?

See daddy? All the keys are in alphabetical order now.

Those who can't write programs, write help files.

'INSERT DISK THREE'? But I can only get two in the drive!

Smash forehead on keyboard to continue ...

Enter any 11-digit prime number to continue ...

The world is coming to an end ... SAVE YOUR BUFFERS!

Computer scientists are programmed to do it by macro insertion.

Working computer hardware is a lot like an erect penis: It stays up as long as you don't fuck with it.

Ban cryptography! Yes. Let's also ban pencils, pens and paper, since criminals can use them to draw plans of the joint they are casing or even, god forbid, create one time pads to pass uncrackable codes to each other. Ban open spaces since criminals could use them to converse with each other out of earshot of the police. Let's ban flags since they could be used to pass secret messages in semaphore. In fact let's just ban all forms of verbal and non-verbal communication—let's see those criminals make plans now!

During the winter my computer doubles as an extra radiator.

Cooling fans generate white noise, which helps me get to sleep.

Who has time for boot sequences?

As long as the computer is running, it's not broken.

Computer doubles as a power failure notification device.

My penis grows 1mm every 5 days of uptime.

Can claim CPU cycles donated to SETI@home, folding@home et al, as charitable donations on my income taxes.

Somebody might say something important on IRC.

Too difficult to find power switch with eye crust.

Around computers it is difficult to find the correct unit of time to measure progress. Some cathedrals took a century to complete. Can you imagine the grandeur and scope of a program that would take as long?

When computer is off, it is no longer protected by the firewall.

A logician trying to explain logic to a programmer is like a cat trying to explain to a fish what it's like to get wet.

Reverse Polish Notation: A method of price justification for expensive calculators.

Q: How many software engineers does it take to change a light-bulb?
A: It can't be done; it's a hardware problem.

If it jams, force it. If it breaks, it needed replacing anyway.

Your program is sick! Shoot it and put it out of its memory.

Dating a girl is just like writing software. Everythings going to work just fine in the testing lab (dating), but as soon as you have contract with a customer (marriage), then your program (life) is going to be facing new situations you never expected. You'll be forced to patch the code (admit you're wrong) and then the code (wife) will just end up all bloated and unmaintainable in the end.

Want to come see my hard drive? I promise it isn't 3.5 inches and it ain't floppy.

When computing, whatever happens, behave as though you meant it to happen.

When you get to the point where you really understand your computer, it's probably obsolete.

The first place to look for information is in the section of the manual where you least expect to find it.

When the going gets tough, upgrade.

Dude, I hate to be the bearer of bad news, but I'm afraid you've been hacked—the FTP server at has all your personal files. See for yourself; just log in with your normal id ...

For every action, there is an equal and opposite malfunction. If the code doesn't bother you, don't bother it.

To err is human ... to blame your computer for your mistakes is even more human, it is downright natural.

The term reboot comes from the Middle Ages (before computers). Horses who stopped in mid-stride required a boot to the rear to start again. Thus the term to rear-boot, later abbreviated into reboot.

He who laughs last probably made a back-up.

BASIC programmers never die, they GOSUB and don't RETURN.

Real programmers don't write in BASIC. Actually, no programmers write in BASIC after reaching puberty.

Profanity is the one language all programmers know best.

Programming software is a constant fight.

'Always apply the latest updates' and 'If it ain't broken, don't fix it' are the two rules of system updating ...

If debugging is the process of removing software bugs, then programming must be the process of putting them in.

When the only tool you own is a hammer, every problem you encounter resembles a nail.

There are 10 kinds of people in the world, those that understand binary and those that don't.

There are 10 kinds of people in the world, those that understand trinary, those that don't, and those that confuse it with binary.

Computers make very fast, very accurate mistakes.

Saying that Windows95 is equal to Macintosh is like finding a potato that looks like Jesus and believing you've witnessed the second coming.

If at first you do not succeed, blame your computer.

The software isn't finished until the last user is dead.

Requirements are like water. They're easier to build on when they're frozen.

A complex system that does not work is invariably found to have evolved from a simpler system that worked just fine.

There comes a time in the history of any project when it becomes necessary to shoot the engineers and begin production.

Since I started programming I make as much errors in real life as I make in my source code.

The number one cause of computer problems is computer solutions.

I have yet to meet a C compiler that is more friendly and easier to use than eating soup with a knife.

If the code is poor quality, have it fixed, don't paper over the problem.

A computer program will always do what you tell it to do, but rarely what you want to do.

All I ever wanted was to see Larry Wall give Bill Gates a Perl necklace.

I know your little 4th grade teacher said there are not stupid questions. She was wrong. This is Usenet.

It's a little-known fact that the Y1K problem caused the Dark Ages.

For us Windows users, reports of new security issues seem to come as often as potholes on an Arkansas highway. Like the potholes, looking for the next one isn't all that interesting or entertaining, but we still have to try to avoid them or at least minimize their impact.

If Google made $1 everytime someone used them to find an answer to a tech support question, they would own Microsoft.

Men think that computers should be referred to as female, just like ships, because:

1. No one but their creator understands their internal logic.

2. The language in which they communicate among themselves is incomprehensible to everyone else.

3. Your smallest mistakes are stored in long term memory for later retrieval.

4. As soon as you make a commitment to one, you spend half your paycheck on accessories for it.

5. Miss a period and they go wild.

---

6. You do the same thing for years, and suddenly it's wrong.

Women think computers are male because:

1. They have lots of data, but are still clueless.

2. They are supposed to solve problems, but half the time they *are* the problem.

3. As soon as you commit to one, you realize that if you had only waited a bit longer, you could have had a better model.

4. To get their attention, you have to 'turn them on'.

5. A big 'power-surge' will knock them out for the rest of the night!

6. It is always necessary to have a backup.

7. They'll do whatever you say if you push the right buttons.

8. Size does matter.

To work on a program with the compiler in debug mode and then to sell it compiling it without the debug option is like learning to swim with floaters and then taking them off to swim across the Atlantic.

The web is a dominatrix. Everywhere I turn, I see little buttons ordering me to Submit.

The problem with computers is they do what you tell them.

Error, no keyboard—press F1 to continue.

How C++ is like teenage sex:

1. It is on everyone's mind all the time.

2. Everyone talks about it all the time.

3. Everyone thinks everyone else is doing it.

4. Almost no one is really doing it.

5. The few who are doing it are:

   (a) Doing it poorly.
   (b) Sure it will be better next time.
   (c) Not practising it safely.

As a computer, I find your faith in technology amusing.

hAS aNYONE sEEN MY cAPSLOCK kEY?

Press CTRL-ALT-DEL now for an IQ test.

The Internet: where men are men, women are men, and children are FBI agents.

Some things Man was never meant to know. For everything else, there's Google.

COBOL programs are an exercise in Artificial Inelegance.

Hacking is like sex. You get in, you get out, and hope that you didn't leave something that can be traced back to you.

Standard are industry's way of codifying obsolescence.

Error: Computer possessed; Load EXOR.SYS? [Y / N]

Sysadmins are the janitors of Information Technology, no matter how much the current crop of adolescents looks up to them like boys in the past admired riverboat pilots and railroad engineers.

Once you've googled every single guy whose last name you remember that you slept with, the Internet sorta becomes a useless tool.

I hope the Q-Tips in that 500 count box I bought last night are Year 2000 compliant, 'cause it'll take me at least three years to get through them all.

A

If brute force doesn't solve your problems, then you aren't using enough.

The NeXT Computer: The hardware makes it a PC, the software makes it a workstation, the unit sales makes it a mainframe.

Failure is not acceptable. It comes bundled with Windows.

This is Linux country. If you listen carefully, you can hear Windows reboot ...

Windows 3.1: The best $89 solitaire game you can buy.

A computer without a Microsoft operating system is like a dog without bricks tied to its head.

Unix is user friendly—it's just picky about its friends.

What goes up must come down. Ask any system administrator.

Whom computers would destroy, they must first drive mad.

Error #152: Windows not found: (C)heer (P)arty (D)ance.

M.A.C.I.N.T.O.S.H: Machine Always Crashes, If Not, The Operating System Hangs.

Intel Inside: The world's most commonly used warning label.

Sped up my XT; ran it on 220v! Works greO?

Intel has announced its next chip: the Repentium.

Pentiums melt in your PC, not in your hand.

The original UNIX solved a problem and solved it well, as did the Roman numeral system, the mercury treatment for syphilis, and carbon paper.

The only thing more dangerous than a hardware guy with a code patch is a programmer with a soldering iron.

All computers wait at the same speed.

There is nothing that a kick in the balls or a pressure on RESET won't solve.

A printer consists of three main parts: the case, the jammed paper tray and the blinking red light.

Isaac Asimov

▶ *American science-fiction writer*

Part of the inhumanity of the computer is that, once it is competently programmed and working smoothly, it is completely honest.

All sorts of computer errors are now turning up. You'd be surprised to know the number of doctors who claim they are treating pregnant men.

I do not fear computers. I fear the lack of them.

Mark Atkinson

▶ *Professor of pathology, immunology and laboratory medicine*

In headlines today, the dreaded KILLFILE virus spread across the country adding 'aol.com' to people's Usenet kill files everywhere. The programmer of the virus still remains anonymous, but has been nominated several times for a Nobel Peace Prize.

Norman Augustine

▶ *President and Chief Executive Officer of Lockheed Martin Co.*

One of the most feared expressions in modern times is 'The computer is down.'

Software is like entropy. It is difficult to grasp, weighs nothing, and obeys the second law of thermodynamics; i.e. it always increases.

Matthew Austern

▶ *American computer scientist*

Of course, the best way to get accurate information on Usenet is to post something wrong and wait for corrections.

Charles Babbage

▶ *English 'father of computing'*

On two occasions I have been asked [by members of Parliament!]: 'Pray, Mr. Babbage, if you put into the machine wrong figures, will the right answers come out?' I am not able rightly to apprehend the kind of confusion of ideas that could provoke such a question.

John Backus

▶ *American computer scientist*

I think conventional languages are for the birds. They're just extensions of the von Neumann computer, and they keep our noses in the dirt of dealing with individual words and computing addresses, and doing all kinds of silly things like that, things that we've picked up from programming for computers; we've built them into programming languages; we've built them into FORTRAN; we've built them in PL/1; we've built them into almost every language.

Henry Baker

▶ *American computer scientist*

Software people would never drive to the office if building engineers and automotive engineers were as cavalier about buildings and autos as the software 'engineer' is about his software.

If buffer overflows are ever controlled, it won't be due to mere crashes, but due to their making systems vulnerable to hackers. Software crashes due to mere incompetence apparently don't raise any eyebrows, because no one wants to fault the incompetent programmer and his incompetent boss.

Richard Barbrook

▶ *Coordinator of the Hypermedia Research Centre, University of Wesminister*

The net is nothing but an inert mass of metal, plastic and sand. We are the only living beings in cyberspace.

John Perry Barlow

▶ *American computer scientist*

In cyberspace, the First Amendment is a local ordinance.

Dave Barry

▶ *American humorist*

User /n./ The word computer professionals use when they mean 'idiot'.

Jeff Batten

▶ *American seismologist*

It took me many years but I have gained access to the root account and have removed the user God.

Jean Baudrillard

▶ *French philosopher*

The sad thing about artificial intelligence is that it lacks artifice and therefore intelligence.

F.L. Bauer

▶ *German computer scientist*

Software engineering is that part of computer science which is too difficult for the computer scientist.

Kent Beck

▶ *American computer scientist*

Optimism is an occupational hazard of programming: Feedback is the treatment.

John Beidler

▶ *American computer scientist*

I will not be a lemming and follow the crowd over the cliff and into the C.

Edward V. Berard

▶ *American computer scientist*

Walking on water and developing software from a specification are easy if both are frozen.

Roger Black

▶ *American magazine designer*

For someone who started in print, the most alarming thing about the Internet is that the reader can publish. It takes a while to remember that we are not broadcasting from on high.

Fred Blechman

▶ *American computer scientist*

Version 1 of any software is full of bugs.
Version 2 fixes all the bugs and is great.
Version 3 adds all the things users ask for,
but hides all the great stuff in Version 2.

Barry Boehm

► *American computer scientist*

Poor management can increase software costs more rapidly than any other factor.

Nathaniel Borenstein

► *American computer scientist*

The most likely way for the world to be destroyed, most experts agree, is by accident. That's where we come in; we're computer professionals. We cause accidents.

It should be noted that no ethically-trained software engineer would ever consent to write a DestroyBaghdad procedure. Basic professional ethics would instead require him to write a DestroyCity procedure, to which Baghdad could be given as a parameter.

Bradley's Bromide

If computers get too powerful, we can organize them into a committee—that will do them in.

Dick Brandon

▶ *American computer scientist*

Documentation is like sex: When it is good, it is very, very good; and when it is bad, it is better than nothing.

Leonard Brandwein

▶ *Israeli computer scientist*

Beware of programmers who carry screwdrivers.

Wernher von Braun

▶ *German rocket engineer*

Man is the best computer we can put aboard a spacecraft ... and the only one that can be mass produced with unskilled labor.

Frederick P. Brooks, Jr.

▶ *American computer scientist*

The programmer, like the poet, works only slightly removed from pure thought-stuff. He builds his castles in the air, from air, creating by exertion of the imagination. Few media of creation are so flexible, so easy to polish and rework, so readily capable of realizing grand conceptual structures.

All programmers are optimists. Perhaps this modern sorcery especially attracts those who believe in happy endings and fairy godmothers. Perhaps the hundreds of nitty frustrations drive away all but those who habitually focus on the end goal.

Perhaps it is merely that computers are young, programmers are younger, and the young are always optimists. But however the selection process works, the result is indisputable: 'This time it will surely run' or 'I just found the last bug.'

Einstein argued that there must be simplified explanations of nature, because God is not capricious or arbitrary. No such faith comforts the software engineer.

Andrew Brown

▶ *English journalist*

The Internet is so big, so powerful and pointless that for some people it is a complete substitute for life.

Multimedia? As far as I'm concerned, it's reading with the radio on!

Gene Brown

▶ *American dramatist*

Foolproof systems don't take into account the ingenuity of fools.

Rita May Brown

▶ *American author*

Computer dating is fine, if you're a computer.

Bill Bryson

▶ *American author*

For a long time it puzzled me how something so expensive, so leading edge, could be so useless, and then it occurred to me that a computer is a stupid machine with the ability to do incredibly smart things, while computer programmers are smart people with the ability to do incredibly stupid things. They are, in short, a perfect match.

Bill Bulko

▶ *American computer scientist*

Artificial intelligence: The art of making computers that behave like the ones in movies.

Nolan Bushnell

▶ *American computer scientist and 'father of the video game industry'*

Sometimes the best engineers come in bodies that can't talk.

Joseph Campbell

▶ *American writer*

Computers are like Old Testament gods; lots of rules and no mercy.

Tom Cargill

▶ *American computer scientist*

The first 90% of the code accounts for the first 90% of the development time ... The remaining 10% of the code accounts for the other 90% of the development time.

Nicholas Carr

▶ *American business writer*

IT is becoming a cost of doing business that must be paid by all but provides distinction to none.

George Carrette

▶ *American computer scientist*

First learn computer science and all the theory. Next develop a programming style. Then forget all that and just hack.

Thou shalt not crucify functionality on the cross of portability.

Joe Celko

▶ *American computer scientist and SQL expert*

Where is the information? Lost in the data. Where is the data? Lost in the #@$%?!& database.

Vinton G. Cerf

▶ *Vice President, Data Architecture, MCI Business Markets*

I'm projecting somewhere between 100 million and 200 million computers [on the Net] by the end of December 2000, and about 300 million users by that same time.

Chris Clark

▶ *American computer scientist*

URLs are the 800 numbers of the 1990's.

Arthur C. Clarke

▶ *American science-fiction writer*

Reading computer manuals without the hardware is as frustrating as reading sex manuals without the software.

Bill Clinton

▶ *42nd US president*

Considering the current sad state of our computer programs, software development is clearly still a black art, and cannot yet be called an engineering discipline.

Ronald Coase

▶ *American economist and Nobel prize lauterate*

If you torture the data enough, it will confess.

James Coates

▶ *American columnist*

There never was a chip, it is said, that Bill Gates couldn't slow down with a new batch of features.

Peter Cochrane

▶ *English software engineer and co-founder of ConceptLabs*

Imagine a school with children that can read or write, but with teachers who cannot, and you have a metaphor of the Information Age in which we live.

Peter Coffee

▶ *American computer scientist and columnist*

If there's one thing that computers do well, it's to make the same mistake uncountable times at inhuman speed.

Peter H. Coffin

▶ *American computer scientist*

UNIX is an operating system, OS/2 is half an operating system, Windows is a shell, and DOS is a boot partition virus.

Rich Cook

▶ *American computer scientist*

Programming today is a race between software engineers striving to build bigger and better idiot-proof programs, and the Universe trying to produce bigger and better idiots. So far, the Universe is winning.

Joseph Costello

▶ *President of Cadence*

I've never met a human being who would want to read 17,000 pages of documentation, and if there was, I'd kill him to get him out of the gene pool.

P.D. Coward

▶ *American computer scientist*

The principle objective of software testing is to give confidence in the software.

Seymour Cray

▶ *Father of the Cray-computers*

The trouble with programmers is that you can never tell what a programmer is doing until it's too late.

Memory is like an orgasm. It's a lot better if you don't have to fake it.

If you were plowing a field, which would you rather use? Two strong oxen or 1024 chickens?

Robert X. Cringely

▶ *Fictitious American journalist*

If the automobile had followed the same development cycle as the computer, a Rolls Royce would today cost $100, get a million miles per gallon, and explode once a year, killing everyone inside.

Ward Cunningham

▶ *American computer scientist and inventor of the WikiWiki concept*

If you don't think carefully, you might think that programming is just typing statements in a programming language.

C3PO

▶ *StarWars robot*

The city's central computer told you? R2D2, you know better than to trust a strange computer!

4 D

Guy Debord

▶ *French situationist philosopher*

It is hardly surprising that children should enthusiastically start their education at an early age with the absolute knowledge of computer science; while they are unable to read, for reading demands making judgements at every line .... Conversation is almost dead, and soon so too will be those who knew how to speak.

Larry DeLuca

▶ *American computer scientist*

I've noticed lately that the paranoid fear of computers becoming intelligent and taking over the world has almost entirely disappeared from the common culture. Near as I can tell, this coincides with the release of MS-DOS.

† Dictionary (Anonymous)

- Computer /n./: A device designed to speed and automate errors.

- Computer geek /n./: An asocial, malodorous, pasty-faced monomaniac with all the personality of a cheese-grater.

- Hardware /n./: The part of the computer that you can kick.

- Maniac /n./: An early computer built by nuts.

- Multitasking /adj./: 3 PCs and a chair with wheels

- PASCAL /n./: A programming language named after a man who would turn over in his grave if he knew about it.

- Pencil and paper /n./: An archaic information storage and transmission device that works by depositing smears of graphite on bleached wood pulp. More recent developments in paper-based technology include improved 'write-once' update devices which use tiny rolling heads similar to mouse balls to deposit colored pigment. All these devices require an operator skilled at so-called 'handwriting' technique. (from Jargon File)

- Program /n./: A magic spell cast over a computer allowing it to turn one's input into error messages. v. tr.- To engage in a pastime similar to banging one's head against a wall, but with fewer opportunities for reward.

- Programmer /n./: A red-eyed, mumbling mammal capable of conversing with inanimate objects.

- Programmer /n./: An organism that turns coffee into software.

- RAM /abr./: Rarely Adequate Memory.

- Release /n./: A set of kludges issued by the manufacturer which clashes with the fixes made by the user since the last release.

- SuperComputer /n./: What it sounded like before you bought it.

- Users /n. plural/: Collective term for those who stare vacently at a monitor. Users are divided into three Types: Novice, Intermediate and Expert:

  - Novice Users: People who are afraid that simply pressing a key might break their computer.
  - Intermediate Users: People who don't know how to fix their computer after pressing a key that broke it.
  - Expert Users: People who break other people's computers.

- Vampireware /n./: A project which is capable of sucking the lifeblood out of anyone unfortunate enough to be assigned to it, which never actually sees the light of day, but nonetheless refuses to die.

Edsger Dijkstra

▶ *American computer scientist*

The art of programming is the art of organizing complexity, of mastering multitude and avoiding its bastard chaos.

The question of whether computers can think is just like the question of whether submarines can swim.

The use of COBOL cripples the mind; its teaching should, therefore, be regarded as a criminal offense.

It is practically impossible to teach good programming style to students that [sic] have had prior exposure to BASIC; as potential programmers they are mentally mutilated beyond hope of regeneration.

Computer science is no more about computers than astronomy is about telescopes.

Please don't fall into the trap of believing that I am terribly dogmatical about [the GOTO statement]. I have the uncomfortable feeling that others are making a religion out of it, as if the conceptual problems of programming could be solved by a single trick, by a simple form of coding discipline!

Projects promoting programming in natural language are intrinsically doomed to fail.

Theodosius Dobzansky

▶ *American biologist*

There is no doubt that human survival will continue to depend more and more on human intellect and technology. It is idle to argue whether this is good or bad. The point of no return was passed long ago, before anyone knew it was happening.

Bob Dole

▶ *Former US vice-president candidate*

The Internet is a great way to get on the net.

K. Eric Drexler

▶ *Researcher, author, and policy advocate, introducing the 'nanotechnology' term*

Replicating assemblers and thinking machines pose basic threats to people and to life on Earth. Among the cognoscenti of nanotechnology, this threat has become known as the gray goo problem.

Peter F. Drucker

▶ *Writer, management consultant and university professor*

The computer actually may have aggravated management's degenerative tendency to focus inward on costs.

Few companies that installed computers to reduce the employment of clerks have realized their expectations ... They now need more, and more expensive clerks even though they call them 'operators' or 'programmers'.

The computer is a moron.

When computers (people) are networked, their power multiplies geometrically. Not only can people share all that information inside their machines, but they can reach out and instantly tap the power of other machines (people), essentially making the entire network their computer.

John C. Dvorak

▶ *Columnist, author, and editor*

In all large corporations, there is a pervasive fear that someone, somewhere is having fun with a computer on company time. Networks help alleviate that fear.

Esther Dyson

▶ *Editor at large at CNET Networks*

It may not always be profitable at first for businesses to be online, but it is certainly going to be unprofitable not to be online.

Sheila M. Eby

▶ *American business executive*

A computer won't clean up the errors in your manual of procedures.

Sir Arthur Eddington

▶ *English astrophysicist*

We are a bit of stellar matter gone wrong. We are physical machinery—puppets that strut and talk and laugh and die as the hand of time pulls the strings beneath. But there is one elementary inescapable answer. We are that which asks the question.

Chester G. Edwards

▶ *American computer scientist*

Let's face the obvious: Yesterday we were nerds, today we're the cognitive elite. Let's conquer.

Paul Ehrlich

▶ *American biologist*

To err is human, but to really foul things up you need a computer.

Lewis D. Eigen

▶ *American author and editor*

The workers and professionals of the world will soon be divided into two distinct groups. Those who will control computers and those who will be controlled by computers. It would be best for you to be in the former group.

T.S. Eliot

▶ *American poet, critic, and editor*

Where is the wisdom? Lost in the knowledge. Where is the knowledge? Lost in the information.

Douglas Engelbart

▶ *American computer scientist*

The digital revolution is far more significant than the invention of writing or even of printing.

Dino Esposito

▶ *Italian computer scientist and editor*

In a world without walls and fences, who needs Windows and Gates?

John Evans

▶ *English author*

The Internet is like a giant jellyfish. You can't step on it. You can't go around it. You've got to get through it.

Jim Fawcette

▶ *President, Fawcette Technical Publications, Inc.*

If software were as unreliable as economic theory, there wouldn't be a plane made of anything other than paper that could get off the ground.

Richard P. Feynman

▶ *American physicist*

There is a computer disease that anybody who works with computers knows about. It's a very serious disease and it interferes completely with the work. The trouble with computers is that you 'play' with them!

Robert Firth

▶ *American computer scientist*

— C++ has it's place in the history of programming languages.
— Just as Caligula has his place in the history of the Roman
Empire?

... one of the main causes of the fall of the Roman Empire
was that, lacking zero, they had no way to indicate successful
termination of their C programs.

Bob Frankston

▶ *American computer scientist*

Reusing pieces of code is liked picking off sentences from other
people's stories and trying to make a magazine article.

Pierre Gallois

▶ *French computer scientist*

If you put tomfoolery into a computer, nothing comes out but
tomfoolery. But this tomfoolery, having passed through a very
expensive machine, is somehow ennobled and no one dares crit-
icize it.

Steven R. Garman

▶ *President & CEO, OI Systems Inc.*

Physics is the universe's operating system.

Laurent Gasser

▶ *Managing director of Personatests.com*

Computers do not solve problems, they execute solutions.

Bill Gates

► *Microsoft founder and CEO*

The first rule of any technology used in a business is that automation applied to an efficient operation will magnify the efficiency. The second is that automation applied to an inefficient operation will magnify the inefficiency.

I don't think there's anything unique about human intelligence. All the neurons in the brain that make up perceptions and emotions operate in a binary fashion.

Be nice to nerds. Chances are you'll end up working for one.

The best way to prepare [to be a programmer] is to write programs, and to study great programs that other people have written. In my case, I went to the garbage cans at the Computer Science Center and fished out listings of their operating system.

A great lathe operator commands several times the wage of an average lathe operator, but a great writer of software code is worth 10,000 times the price of an average software writer.

Microsoft's only factory asset is the human imagination.

640K ought to be enough for anybody. (1981)

Louis Gerstner

► *Chairman and CEO, IBM*

Computers are magnificent tools for the realization of our dreams, but no machine can replace the human spark of spirit, compassion, love, and understanding.

William Gibson

▶ *American science-fiction writer*

The Net is a waste of time, and that's exactly what's right about it.

John Gilmore

▶ *American computer scientist*

The Net interprets censorship as damage and routes around it.

Paul Gilster

▶ *American free-lance writer*

Your pathway through its passages is determined by your mouse click, making your experience of hypertext a malleable and personalized phenomenon.

J.H. Goldfuss

▶ *American computer scientist*

There is only one satisfying way to boot a computer.

Zachary Good

▶ *American programmer*

I sit looking at this damn computer screen all day long, day in and day out, week after week, and think: Man, if I could just find the 'on' switch ...

Al Goodman

▶ *American programmer*

The perfect computer has been developed. You just feed in your problems and they never come out again.

Rick Gordon

▶ *American computer scientist*

Crossposting isn't inherently evil, in the same sense that, say, necrophilia doesn't really hurt anybody. One wonders only whether it's appropriate to the occasion.

Steven Gordon

▶ *Australian computer scientist*

Part of the reason so many companies continue to develop software using variations of waterfall is the misconception that the analysis phase of waterfall completes the design and the rest of the process is just non-creative execution of programming skills.

Paul Graham

▶ *American programmer and essayist*

The object-oriented model makes it easy to build up programs by accretion. What this often means, in practice, is that it provides a structured way to write spaghetti code.

Bob Gray

▶ *American computer scientist*

Writing in C or C++ is like running a chain saw with all the safety guards removed.

Philip Greenspun

▶ *American software engineer*

BestOfBreed solutions: A bunch of inferior programs huddling together for warmth around the dying embers of Windows NT.

George Greenstein

▶ *American astronomer*

I went on to test the program in every way I could devise. I strained it to expose its weaknesses. I ran it for high-mass stars and low-mass stars, for stars born exceedingly hot and those born relatively cold. I ran it assuming the superfluid currents beneath the crust to be absent—not because I wanted to know the answer, but because I had developed an intuitive feel for the answer in this particular case. Finally I got a run in which the computer showed the pulsar's temperature to be less than absolute zero. I had found an error. I chased down the error and fixed it. Now I had improved the program to the point where it would not run at all.

Greer's Third Law

A computer program does what you tell it to do, not what you want it to do.

Vartan Gregorian

▶ *President, N.Y. Public Library*

The book is here to stay. What we're doing is symbolic of the peaceful co-existence of the book and the computer.

Doug Gwyn

▶ *American computer scientist*

UNIX was not designed to stop people from doing stupid things, because that would also stop them from doing clever things.

8 H

Katie Hafner

▶ *American reporter for New York Times*

How would a car function if it were designed like a computer? Occasionally, executing a maneuver would cause your car to stop and fail and you would have to re-install the engine, and the airbag system would say, 'Are you sure?' before going off.

Mark Halpern

▶ *American astro-physicist*

That tendency to err that programmers have been noticed to share with other human beings has often been treated as though it were an awkwardness attendant upon programming's adolescence, which like acne would disappear with the craft's coming of age. It has proved otherwise.

Harold Hambrose

► *President of Electronic Ink*

I find sitting at a specially equipped desk in front of some pretty ugly plastics and staring at a little window is a very unnatural event.

Scott Hammer

► *American software engineer*

If it's there and you can see it—it's real.
If it's not there and you can see it—it's virtual.
If it's there and you can't see it—it's transparent.
If it's not there and you can't see it—you erased it!

Stephen Hawking

► *American physicist*

I think computer viruses should count as life. I think it says something about human nature that the only form of life we have created so far is purely destructive. We've created life in our own image.

Unless mankind redesigns itself by changing our DNA through altering our genetic make-up, computer-generated robots will take over our world.

LeMel Hebert-Williams

▶ *American computer artist*

Kids today have so many advantages I never had. There's no telling what I could've accomplished with a home computer and a handgun.

Juuso Heimonen

▶ *Finnish computer programmer*

You know you're a geek when ... You try to shoo a fly away from the monitor with your cursor. That just happened to me. It was scary.

Robert A. Heinlein

▶ *American science-fiction writer*

Don't explain computers to laymen. Simpler to explain sex to a virgin.

Joshua Heller

▶ *American computer scientist*

Usenet is like Tetris for people who still remember how to read.

Tony Hoare

▶ *English computer scientist*

Pointers are like jumps, leading wildly from one part of the data structure to another. Their introduction into high-level languages has been a step backwards from which we may never recover.

There are two ways of constructing a software design. One way is to make it so simple that there are obviously no deficiencies. And the other way is to make it so complicated that there are no obvious deficiencies.

Oliver Wendell Holmes

▶ *American author and physician*

What a satire, by the way, is that machine [Babbage's Engine], on the mere mathematician! A Frankenstein-monster, a thing without brains and without heart, too stupid to make a blunder; that turns out results like a corn-sheller, and never grows any wiser or better, though it grinds a thousand bushels of them!

Grace Hopper

▶ *American computer scientist*

I had a running compiler and nobody would touch it. They told me computers could only do arithmetic.

Blair Houghton

▶ *American author*

Come to think of it, there are already a million monkeys on a million typewriters, and Usenet is NOTHING like Shakespeare.

I must've seen it in a Usenet posting; that's sort of like hearsay evidence from Richard Nixon ...

Elbert Hubbard

▶ *American author*

One machine can do the work of fifty ordinary men. No machine can do the work of one extraordinary man.

Robert Hummel

▶ *American computer scientist*

Fast, fat computers breed slow, lazy programmers.

IBM Maintenance Manual

► *International Business Machine*

All parts should go together without forcing. You must remember that the parts you are reassembling were disassembled by you. Therefore, if you can't get them together again, there must be a reason. By all means, do not use a hammer. (1925)

Andy G. Ihnatko

► *American computer scientist*

Windows95: It's like upgrading from Reagan to Bush.

Joseph Jesson

▶ *American computer programmer*

The first step is to decide what Internet services users need to access and limit their access to those services.

Penn Jillett

▶ *American author*

My favorite thing about the Internet is that you get to go into the private world of real creeps without having to smell them.

Steve Jobs

▶ *CEO and co-founder of Apple Computer, Inc.*

So we went to Atari and said, 'Hey, we've got this amazing thing, even built with some of your parts, and what do you think about funding us? Or we'll give it to you. We just want to do it. Pay our salary, we'll come work for you.' And they said, 'No'. So then we went to Hewlett-Packard, and they said, 'Hey, we don't need you. You haven't got through college yet'.

Ralph Johnson

▶ *American computer scientist*

Before software can be reusable it first has to be usable.

Stephen C. Johnson

▶ *American mathematician and programmer*

Using TSO is like kicking a dead whale down the beach.

Bertil Jonell

▶ *Swedish mathematician and programmer*

It can be shown that for any nutty theory, beyond-the-fringe political view or strange religion there exists a proponent on the Net. The proof is left as an exercise for your KILLFILE.

Howard Mumford Jones

▶ *American critic and educator*

Ours is the age which is proud of machines that think and suspicious of men who try to.

Bill Joy

▶ *American engineer and co-founder of Sun Microsystems*

I fear the the new object-oriented systems may suffer the fate of LISP, in that they can do many things, but the complexity of the class hierarchies may cause them to collapse under their own weight.

Rich Julius

► *American computer scientist and former president of STC*

An idiot with a computer is a faster, better idiot.

Mitchell Kapor

▶ *American computer scientist and founder of Lotus Development Corporation*

Getting information off the Internet is like taking a drink from a fire hydrant.

Spencer Katt

▶ *American computer journalist*

A friend of the Feline reports that Big Blue marketing and sales personnel have been strictly forbidden to use the word 'mainframe'. Instead, in an attempt to distance themselves from the dinosaur, they're to use the more PC-friendly phrase 'large enterprise server'. If that's the case, the Katt retorted, they should also refer to 'dumb terminals' as 'intelligence-challenged workstations'.

Alan Kay

▶ *American computer scientist*

The protean nature of the computer is such that it can act like a machine or like a language to be shaped and exploited.

William M. Kelly

▶ *American computer scientist*

Man is a slow, sloppy and brilliant thinker; the machine is fast, accurate and stupid.

Stan Kelly-Bootle

▶ *English freelance programmer, consultant and writer*

Computer science:

1. A study akin to numerology and astrology, but lacking the precision of the former and the success of the latter.

2. The boring art of coping with a large number of trivialities.

Should array indices start at 0 or 1? My compromise of 0.5 was rejected without, I thought, proper consideration.

John F. Kennedy

▶ *35th American president*

Man is still the most extraordinary computer of all.

Brian Kernigan

▶ *American computer scientist*

Controlling complexity is the essence of computer programming.

Donald Knuth

▶ *Author of* TEX

Beware of bugs in the above code; I have only proved it correct, not tried it.

Rich Kulawiec

▶ *American computer scientist*

Any sufficiently advanced bug is indistinguishable from a feature.

Neil Kurshan

▶ *American rabbi*

Family life is not a computer program that runs on its own; it needs continual input from everyone.

Leslie Lamport

▶ *American mathematician and computer scientist*

A distributed system is one in which the failure of a computer you didn't even know existed can render your own computer unusable.

Doug Larson

▶ *American author*

Home computers are being called upon to perform many new functions, including the consumption of homework which was formerly eaten by the dog.

Matt Larson

▶ *American computer scientist and author*

If you can't beat your computer at chess, do what I did—try kick-boxing.

Laws of Computer Programming

1. Any given program, when running, is obsolete.

2. Any given program costs more and takes longer.

3. If a program is useful, it will have to be changed.

4. If a program is useless, it will have to be documented.

5. Any program will expand to fill available memory.

6. The value of a program is proportional to the weight of its output.

7. Program complexity grows until it exceeds the capabilities of the programmer who must maintain it.

8. Any non-trivial program contains at least one bug.

9. Undetectable errors are infinite in variety, in contrast to detectable errors, which by definition are limited.

10. Adding manpower to a late software project makes it later.

Paul Leary

▶ *American musician*

That's what's cool about working with computers. They don't argue, they remember everything and they don't drink all your beer.

Karl Lehenbauer

▶ *NeoSoft technical director*

Voodoo Programming: Things programmers do that they know shouldn't work but they try anyway, and which sometimes actually work, such as recompiling everything.

Tom Lehrer

▶ *American songwriter, satirist, pianist, mathematician*

Counting in octal is just like counting in decimal—if you don't use your thumbs.

Steven Levy

▶ *American journalist and author*

Though the grammars, aesthetics, and even the jargon of this rather ephemeral art form have yet to be fixed, there is a quiet understanding among those working in the front lines of software design that they are participating in the most vital means of expression in our time.

Chris Lipe

▶ *American computer scientist*

I don't understand why cheerleaders won't talk to me. Maybe I don't throw five touchdowns against Newport High, but let's see one of those football morons program in assembly language!

Bill Lye

▶ *American computer scientist*

If you sat a monkey down in front of a keyboard, the first thing typed would be a UNIX command.

James Magary

▶ *American computer scientist*

Computers can figure out all kinds of problems, except the things in the world that just don't add up.

Jim McCarthy

▶ *Principal, McCarthy Communications*

Burn-out in a developer is the death of the artistic self, a perverse maturation, a shrinking with age, a withering with experience.

Herbert Marshall McLuhan

▶ *American author*

The global village is not created by the motor car or even by the airplane. Its created by instant electronic information movement.

Edward Shepherd Mead

▶ *American author*

Not even computers will replace committees, because committees buy computers.

Joseph Menn

▶ *American writer*

Suffusing [the technology] culture is the belief among programmers and engineers that they're working on the Next Big Thing projects that change the world, not just deliver a more absorbent diaper or crunchier breakfast cereal.

Bertrand Meyer

▶ *American computer scientist and author*

You can either have software quality or you can have pointer arithmetic, but you cannot have both at the same time.

Mark Minasi

▶ *American technology writer and speaker*

If McDonalds were run like a software company, one out of every hundred Big Macs would give you food poisoning—and the response would be, 'We're sorry, here's a coupon for two more.'

Marvin Minsky

▶ *American computer scientist and author*

It's ridiculous to live 100 years and only be able to remember 30 million bytes. You know less than a compact disc. The human condition is really becoming more obsolete every minute.

I bet the human brain is a kluge.

MIT

▶ *Massachusettes Institute of Technology*

Applicants must also have extensive knowledge of UNIX, although they should have sufficiently good programming taste to not consider this an achievement. (MIT job advertisement)

Olav Mjelde

▶ *Norwegian computer scientist*

Bugs—'They don't make bugs like Bunny anymore.'

Elting Elmore Morison

▶ *American author*

The computer is no better than its program.

Walter Mossberg

▶ *American columnist*

Just remember: You're not a dummy, no matter what those computer books claim. The real dummies are the people who, though technically expert, couldn't design hardware and software that's usable by normal consumers if their lives depended upon it.

Why shouldn't a PC work like a refrigerator or a toaster?

Patrick Murray

▶ *American computer scientist*

The trouble with the Internet is that it's replacing masturbation as a leisure activity.

Edward R. Murrow

▶ *American broadcast journalist*

The newest computer can merely compound, at speed, the oldest problem in the relations between human beings, and in the end the communicator will be confronted with the old problem, of what to say and how to say it.

Eric Naggum

▶ *American computer scientist*

For the time being, programming is a consumer job, assembly line coding is the norm, and what little exciting stuff is being performed is not going to make it compared to the mass-marketed crap sold by those who think they can surf on the previous half-century's worth of inventions forever.

NASA

▶ *National Aeronautics and Space Administration*

Man is the lowest-cost, 150-pound, nonlinear, all-purpose computer system which can be mass-produced by unskilled labor.

Roger Needham

▶ *American computer scientist*

If you think encryption solves your security problems then you don't understand encryption and you don't understand security.

The best research is done with a shovel, not tweezers.

Nicholas P. Negroponte

▶ *American educator and columnist*

It's not computer literacy that we should be working on, but sort of human-literacy. Computers have to become human-literate.

Ted Nelson

▶ *American computer scientist*

A computer is essentially a trained squirrel: Acting on reflex, thoughtlessly running back and forth and storing away nuts until some other stimulus makes it do something else.

Larry Niven

▶ *American science-fiction author*

That's the thing about people who think they hate computers. What they really hate is lousy programmers.

Michael O'Brien

► *American artist and author*

A sysadmin's life is a sorry one. The only advantage he has over Emergency Room doctors is that malpractice suits are rare. On the other hand, ER doctors never have to deal with patients installing new versions of their own innards!

James O'Donnell

► *Provost of Georgetown University*

There are Medieval manuscript books that may have lain unread for hundreds of years, but offered their treasures to the first reader who found and tried them. An electronic text subjected to the same neglect is unlikely to survive five years.

Ken Olson

▶ *President, chairman and founder of Digital Equipment Corp.*

There is no reason anyone would want a computer in their home. (1977)

Robert Orben

▶ *American humorist*

To err is human—and to blame it on a computer is even more so.

Tim O'Reilly

▶ *American computer writer*

Anyone who puts a small gloss on a fundamental technology, calls it proprietary, and then tries to keep others from building on it, is a thief.

Andrew Orlowski

▶ *English columnist*

See, no matter how clever your automation systems might be, it all falls apart if your human wetware isn't up to the job.

Tom Ostad

▶ *Norwegian author*

I rigged my cellular to send a message to my PDA, which is online with my PC, to get it to activate the voicemail, which sends the message to the inbox of my email, which routes it to the PDA, which beams it back to the cellular. Then I realized my gadgets have a better social life than I do.

Heinz Pagels

▶ *American physicist*

We may begin to see reality differently simply because the computer ... provides a different angle on reality.

Parkinson's Law of Data

Data expands to fill the space available for storage.

James "Kibo" Parry

▶ *American Usenet user*

Usenet is a Mobius strand of spaghetti.

Remember, on Prodigy, the users are stupid enough that they may only be allowed to see intelligent, mature posts; who decided this was most appropriate for their reading level? Over here on the Real Net, we're as infantile as we wanna be and we're all geniuses. I can say whatever I want because I know that everyone with a brain will simply ignore me completely. As John Cleese said, this will offend precisely those people who *should* be offended.

John Allen Paulos

► *American mathematician and author*

The Internet is the world's largest library. It's just that all the books are on the floor.

Bruce Perens

► *American author*

Programmers are like artists. Writing software that just gets put away feels like intellectual masturbation.

Marko Peric

▶ *American editor*

If the Internet is a superhighway, then AOL must be a fleet of farm equipment that straddles five lanes and pays no heed to 'Keep Right Except to Pass' signs.

Alan Perlis

▶ *American computer scientist*

I think it is inevitable that people program poorly. Training will not substantially help matters. We have to learn to live with it.

The computing field is always in need of new cliches.

Jeff Pesis

▶ *American author*

Hardware: The parts of a computer that can be kicked.

Pablo Picasso

▶ *Spanish painter*

Computers are useless. They can only give you answers.

John Pierce

▶ *American heldentenor*

After growing wildly for years, the field of computing appears
to be reaching its infancy.

Andy Pierson

▶ *American scholar*

We will never become a truly paper-less society until the Palm
Pilot folks come out with WipeMe 1.0.

Dave Platt

▶ *American computer scientist*

Managing senior programmers is like herding cats.

Steve Polyak

▶ *American computer scientist*

Before we work on artificial intelligence why don't we do something about natural stupidity?

Popular Mechanics

▶ *American Magazine*

Computers in the future may weigh no more than 1.5 tons. (1949)

Eric Porterfield

▶ *American computer scientist*

The most overlooked advantage to owning a computer is that if they foul up, there's no law against whacking them around a little.

Neil Postman

▶ *American author*

Computers are merely ingenious devices to fulfill unimportant functions. The computer revolution is an explosion of nonsense.

Lawrence Clark Powell

▶ *American librarian and author*

We are the children of a technological age. We have found streamlined ways of doing much of our routine work. Printing is no longer the only way of reproducing books. Reading them, however, has not changed ...

Thomas Pynchon

▶ *American writer*

If patterns of ones and zeros were like patterns of human lives and death, if everything about an individual could be represented in a computer record by a long string of ones and zeros, then what kind of creature would be represented by a long string of lives and deaths?

17

QuickLaunch

If I ever did a quick launch with my computer, I guess I still wouldn't know it.

Mitch Radcliffe

▶ *Writer and internet developer*

A computer lets you make more mistakes faster than any invention in human history—with the possible exceptions of handguns and tequila.

Jef Raskin

▶ *Creator of Macintosh computer at Apple Computer, Inc.*

Imagine if every Thursday your shoes exploded if you tied them the usual way. This happens to us all the time with computers, and nobody thinks of complaining.

Wayne Ratliffe

▶ *Author of dBASE*

Management would rather have 99% of $100,000,000 instead of 95% of $300,000,000 because 99% sounds better than 95%.

Waldi Ravens

▶ *American computer scientist*

A C program is like a fast dance on a newly waxed dance floor by people carrying razors.

Eric Raymond

▶ *American internet developer*

Being a social outcast helps you stay concentrated on the really important things, like thinking and hacking.

Computer science education cannot make anybody an expert programmer any more than studying brushes and pigment can make somebody an expert painter.

Brian K. Reid

▶ *American computer scientist*

In computer science, we stand on each other's feet.

Janet Reno

▶ *78th American attorney general*

They have computers, and they may have other weapons of mass destruction.

At this time I do not have a personal relationship with a computer.

Denise Richards

▶ *American actress*

The Internet's been so great, and it's so nice to have fans do nice, elaborate websites, but I think the downside is some of the things ... for real fans to go on and see that 90 percent of the information isn't true or to see pictures that aren't really me, or for them to be able to sell these things, that's one of the downsides, I think.

Dennis Ritchie

▶ *American computer scientist, author of UNIX*

UNIX is basically a simple operating system, but you have to be a genius to understand the simplicity.

Andy Rooney

▶ *CBS news correspondent*

Computers make it easier to do a lot of things, but most of the things they make it easier to do don't need to be done.

Michael Rothschild

▶ *President, CEO and founder of Maxager Technology*

Since the invention of the microprocessor, the cost of moving a byte of information around has fallen on the order of 10-million-fold. Never before in the human history has any product or service gotten 10 million times cheaper-much less in the course of a couple decades. That's as if a 747 plane, once at $150 million a piece, could now be bought for about the price of a large pizza.

Neil J. Rubenking

▶ *Writer and project leader for PC Magazine*

Writing the first 90 percent of a computer program takes 90 percent of the time. The remaining ten percent also takes 90 percent of the time and the final touches also take 90 percent of the time.

Jeff Scholnik

► *American computer scientist*

Who cares how it works, just as long as it gives the right answer?

Norm Schryer

► *American engineer*

If the code and the comments disagree, then both are probably wrong.

John Searle

► *American philosopher*

The reason that no computer program can ever be a mind is simply that a computer program is only syntactical, and minds are more than syntactical. Minds are semantical, in the sense that they have more than a formal structure, they have a content.

Peter Seebach

▶ *American free-lance writer*

A hacker on a roll may be able to produce, in a period of a few months, something that a small development group (say, 7-8 people) would have a hard time getting together over a year. IBM used to report that certain programmers might be as much as 100 times as productive as other workers, or more.

Claude Shannon

▶ *American mathematical engineer, father of information theory*

I visualize a time when we will be to robots what dogs are to humans, and I'm rooting for the machines.

Charles Simony

▶ *American computer scientist*

XML is not a language in the sense of a programming language any more than sketches on a napkin are a language.

Beryl Simpson

▶ *American employment counselor*

My job as a reservationist was very routine, computerized ... I had no free will. I was just part of that stupid computer.

Homer Simpson

▶ *Cartoon figure*

The Internet? Is that thing still around?

M.G. Siriam

▶ *American critic*

Looking at the proliferation of personal web pages on the net, it looks like very soon everyone on Earth will have 15 Megabytes of fame.

B.F. Skinner

▶ *American psychologist*

The real problem is not whether machines think but whether men do.

Disclaimer: These opiini^H^H damn! ^H^H ^Q ^[.... :w :q :wq :wq! ^d X ^? exit X Q ^C ^? :quitbye CTRL-ALT-DEL ~~q :~q logout save/quit :!QUIT ^[zz ^[ZZZZZZ ^H man vi ^^L ^[c ^# ^E ^X ^I ^T ? help helpquit ^D ^d man help ^C ^c help ?Quit ?q CTRL-SHFT-DEL. Hey, what does this button d ...

Joseph Snip

▶ *American writer*

The real problem is not whether machines think but whether men do.

Robert Solow

▶ *American economist*

I can see computers everywhere—except in the productivity statistics!

Gene Spafford

▶ *American computer scientist*

Axiom 1: The Usenet is not the real world. The Usenet usually does not even resemble the real world.

Corollary 1: Attempts to change the real world by altering the structure of the Usenet is an attempt to work sympathetic magic—electronic voodoo.

Corollary 2: Arguing about the significance of newsgroup names and their relation to the way people really think is equivalent to arguing whether it is better to read tea leaves or chicken entrails to divine the future.

Axiom 2: Ability to type on a computer terminal is no guarantee of sanity, intelligence, or commonsense.

Corollary 3: An infinite number of monkeys at an infinite number of keyboards could produce something like Usenet.

Corollary 4: They could do a better job of it.

Axiom 3: Sturgeon's Law (90% of everything is crap) applies to Usenet.

Corollary 5: In an unmoderated newsgroup, no one can agree on what constitutes the 10%.

Corollary 6: Nothing guarantees that the 10% isn't crap, too.

Usenet is like a herd of performing elephants with diarrhea—massive, difficult to redirect, awe-inspiring, entertaining, and a source of mind-boggling amounts of excrement when you least expect it.

Herbert Spencer

▶ *American computer scientist*

We're thinking about upgrading from SunOS 4.1.1 to SunOS 3.5.

Thou shalt not follow the NULL pointer, for chaos and madness await thee at its end.

Richard Stallman

▶ *American computer scientist, founder of the GNU project*

In 1971 when I joined the staff of the MIT Artificial Intelligence Lab, all of us who helped develop the operating system software, we called ourselves hackers.

Rob Stampfli

▶ *American computer scientist*

If addiction is judged by how long a dumb animal will sit pressing a lever to get a 'fix' of something, to its own detriment, then I would conclude that netnews is far more addictive than cocaine.

Star Trek

▶ *Science-fiction movie and TV-show*

Kirk: Do you want to know something? Everybody's human.
Spock: I find that remark insulting.

Scotty: She's all yours, sir. All systems automated and ready. A chimpanzee and two trainees could run her!
Kirk: Thank you, Mr. Scott, I'll try not to take that personally.

Guy Steele

▶ *American engineer*

If the programmer can simulate a construct faster than a compiler can implement the construct itself, then the compiler writer has blown it badly.

Peter Steiner

▶ *American cartoonist*

On the Internet, nobody knows you're a dog.

Neal Stephenson

▶ *American author*

Once the Invisible Hand has taken all the historical inequities and smeared them out into a broad global layer of what a Pakistani brickmaker would consider to be prosperity—y'know what? There's only four things we do better than anyone else: music, movies, microcode (software), and high-speed pizza delivery.

Bruce Sterling

▶ *American science-fiction writer*

I have no sustained relationship with any person whom I've met only by and through Email ... I uncharitably speculate that it's because I already have a life.

I used to think that cyberspace was fifty years away. What I thought was fifty years away, was only ten years away. And what I thought was ten years away ... it was already here. I just wasn't aware of it yet.

Clifford Stoll

▶ *American author*

Treat your password like your toothbrush. Don't let anybody else use it, and get a new one every six months.

Why is it drug addicts and computer afficionados are both called users?

Spending an evening on the World Wide Web is much like sitting down to a dinner of Cheetos, two hours later your fingers are yellow and you're no longer hungry, but you haven't been nourished.

Charles M. Strauss

▶ *American computer scientist*

Mostly, when you see programmers, they aren't doing anything. One of the attractive things about programmers is that you cannot tell whether or not they are working simply by looking at them. Very often they're sitting there seemingly drinking coffee and gossiping, or just staring into space. What the programmer is trying to do is get a handle on all the individual and unrelated ideas that are scampering around in his head.

Bjarne Stroustrup

▶ *Danish computer scientist*

There's an old story about the person who wished his computer were as easy to use as his telephone. That wish has come true, since I no longer know how to use my telephone.

To many managers, getting rid of the arrogant, undisciplined, over-paid, technology-obsessed, improperly-dressed etc. programmers would appear to be a significant added benefit.

An organisation that treats its programmers as morons will soon have programmers that are willing and able to act like morons only.

C makes it easy to shoot yourself in the foot. C++ makes it harder, but when you do, it blows away your whole leg.

There are only two kinds of programming languages: those people always bitch about and those nobody uses.

Andrew Tannenbaum

▶ *American software engineer*

The nice thing about standards is that there are so many of them to choose from.

George Teschner

▶ *American philosopher*

The essence of the computer is not electronic. Computers can be made from toothpicks and bottlecaps, or toilet paper and pebbles.

Lewis Thomas

▶ *American physician, poet, etymologist, and essayist*

The cloning of humans is on most of the lists of things to worry about from science, along with behaviour control, genetic engineering, transplanted heads, computer poetry and the unrestrained growth of plastic flowers.

Christopher Thompson

▶ *American computer scientist*

Sometimes it pays to stay in bed on Monday, rather than spending the rest of the week debugging Monday's code.

Ken Thompson

▶ *American computer scientist, co-author of UNIX*

I just hate to be pushed around by some fucking machine.

FORTRAN was the language of choice for the same reason that three-legged races are popular.

Linus Torvalds

▶ *Finnish computer scientist and author of Linux*

Technical people are better off not looking at patents. If some-body sues you, you change the algorithm or you just hire a hit-man to whack the stupid git.

See, you not only have to be a good coder to create a system like Linux, you have to be a sneaky bastard, too.

Software is like sex: It's better when it's free.

Real men don't use back-ups, they post their stuff on a public FTP-server and let the rest of the world make copies.

The memory management on the PowerPC can be used to frighten small children.

Simon Travaglia

▶ *American computer scientist and author*

Anti-glare screens to prevent eye strain??? In my day, you did-n't need an anti-glare screen. With the power they consumed, when you turned your computer on, the whole building dark-ened!

Maintenance Contractors always dress up nice, with a tie and everything because they believe that a customer will trust a nicely dressed guy with their million dollar equipment just be-cause he's got a nice tie ...

Donald Trump

▶ *American philantropist*

A friend called me up the other day and talked about investing in a dot-com that sells lobsters. Internet lobsters. Where will this end? The next day he sent me a huge package of lobsters on ice. How low can you stoop?

Alan Turing

▶ *English computer scientist*

We shall do a much better programming job, provided we approach the task with a full appreciation of its tremendous difficulty, provided that we respect the intrinsic limitations of the human mind and approach the task as very humble programmers.

Sherry Turkle

▶ *American sociologist and psychologist*

One thing is certain: The riddle of mind, long a topic for philosophers, has taken on new urgency. Under pressure from the computer, the question of mind in relation to machine is becoming a central cultural preoccupation. It is becoming for us what sex was to the Victorians-threat and obsession, taboo and fascination.

Ellen Ullman

▶ *American software engineer and author*

The programmer, who needs clarity, who must talk all day to a machine that demands declarations, hunkers down into a low-grade annoyance. It is here that the stereotype of the programmer, sitting in a dim room, growling from behind Coke cans, has its origins. The disorder of the desk, the floor; the yellow Post-It notes everywhere; the whiteboards covered with scrawl: All this is the outward manifestation of the messiness of human thought. The messiness cannot go into the program; it piles up around the programmer.

Jerry Vuoso

▶ *American computer scientist*

Email: When it absolutely, positively has to get lost at the speed of light.

Vic Vyssotsky

▶ *American mathematician and computer scientist*

Twenty percent of all input forms filled by people contain bad data.

John Walker

▶ *American programmer and co-designer of AutoCAD*

There is a difference between eating a varied diet and chowing down on a cup of lard and sugar once a day. Programmers know this instinctively: They balance their daily menu among the four major food groups: caffeine, sugar, grease, and salt.

Larry Wall

▶ *Programmer, linguist, author and inventor of PERL*

Real programmers can write assembly code in any language.

Computer language design is just like a stroll in the park. Jurassic Park, that is.

Nathan Walton

▶ *American author*

There is unexpected beauty hidden everywhere in this world—
one just has to be open to seeing it. Remember that the next
time you sneeze on your monitor.

Kevin Warwick

▶ *English computer scientist*

On Human Consciousness: John Searle put forward the view
that a shoe is not conscious therefore a computer cannot be
conscious. By the same sort of analogy though, a cabbage is
not conscious therefore a human cannot be conscious.

On Machine Intelligence: Our robots have roughly the equivalent of 50 to 100 brain cells. That means they are about as
intelligent as a slug or a snail or a Manchester United supporter.

An actual robot walking machine which takes one step and then
falls over is worth far more than a computer simulation of 29,000
robots running the London Marathon in record time.

When comparing human memory and computer memory it is
clear that the human version has two distinct disadvantages.
Firstly, as indeed I have experienced myself, due to ageing, human memory can exhibit very poor short term recall.

Thomas Watson

▶ *Former chairman of IBM*

I think there is a world market for maybe five computers. (1943)

Gerald Weinberg

▶ *American author and consultant on software development*

Writing code has a place in the human hierarchy worth somewhere above grave robbing and beneath managing.

Harry Weinberger

▶ *American writer*

If builders built buildings the way programmers wrote programs, then the first woodpecker that came along would destroy civilization.

Bill Weinman

▶ *American author and programmer*

Computers are obstinate about precision. Miss a period here or a semicolon there, and you'll get pistachios instead of caviar every time.

Joseph Weizenbaum

▶ *American computer scientist, Professor Emeritus MIT*

Their rumpled clothes, their unwashed and unshaven faces, and their uncombed hair all testify that they are oblivious to their bodies and to the world in which they move. These are computer bums, compulsive programmers. (1976)

The computer programmer is a creator of universes for which he alone is responsible. Universes of virtually unlimited complexity can be created in the form of computer programs.

Maurice Vincent Wilkes

▶ *English computer scientist*

As soon as we started programming, we found to our surprise that it wasn't as easy to get programs right as we had thought. Debugging had to be discovered. I can remember the exact instant when I realized that a large part of my life from then on was going to be spent in finding mistakes in my own programs.

Pete Wilson

▶ *Former California Governor*

The advent of electronic mail has provided people throughout the world with an expedient and cost-effective means of communication. Unfortunately, it has also created a whole new territory for the high-tech version of the door-to-door salesman.

Steve Wozniak

▶ *American computer scientist, co-founder of Apple Computer, Inc.*

Never trust a computer you can't throw out a window.

Lu Xun

▶ *Chinese satirist and author*

To be suspicious is not a fault. To be suspicious all the time without coming to a conclusion is the defect.

Ed Yourdon

▶ *American computer scientist*

There is nothing in the programming field more despicable than an undocumented program.

If you think your management doesn't know what it's doing or that your organisation turns out low-quality software crap that embarrasses you, then leave.

Jamie Zawinski

▶ *Former Netscape programmer*

Some people, when confronted with a problem, think 'I know, I'll use regular expressions.' Now they have two problems.

Elizabeth Zwicky

▶ *Senior system administrator at Silicon Graphics and president of SAGE (the System Administrators Guide)*

Anyone who has attended a USENIX conference in a fancy hotel can tell you that a sentence like 'You're one of those computer people, aren't you?' is roughly equivalent to 'Look, another amazingly mobile form of slime mold!' in the mouth of a hotel cocktail waitress.

The only thing more frightening than a programmer with a screwdriver or a hardware engineer with a program is a user with a pair of wire cutters and the root password.

Dictionary of OnLine Short-Hands

——————— A

AAMOF	....	As A Matter Of Fact
ADN	....	Any Day Now
AFAIC	....	As Far As I'm Concerned
AFAIK	....	As Far As I Know
AFAIR	....	As Far As I Remember
AFJ	....	April Fools Joke
AFK	....	Away From the Keyboard
AISI	....	As I See It
ANFAWFOS	......	And Now For A Word From Our Sponsor
ANFSCD	.....	And Now For Something Completely Different
AS	....	Another Subject
ASAP	....	As Soon As Possible
ATSL	....	Along The Same Line
AWC	....	After While, Crocodile
AYOR	....	At Your Own Risk

A-OLs .... Administrators OnLine

──────── B

B4N .... Bye For Now

BAK .... Back At Keyboard

BBFN .... Bye Bye For Now

BBIAB .... Be Back In A Bit

BBIAF .... Be Back In A Few (minutes)

BBL .... Be Back Later

BBR .... Burnt Beyond Repair

BCNU .... Be Seein' You

BEG .... Big Evil Grin

BF .... Boy Friend

BFN .... Bye For Now

BION .... Believe It Or Not

BOT .... Back On Topic

BRB .... Be Right Back

BRS .... Big Red Switch

BTA .... But Then Again

BTAIM .... Be That As It May

BTHOM .... Beats The Hell Outta Me

BTOBD .... Be There Or Be Dead

BTW .... By The Way

BWL .... Bursting With Laughter

BWQ .... Buzz Word Quotient

BYE?	'Ready to say goodbye?'
BYKT	But You Knew That
BYOB	Bring Your Own Bottle
BYOM	Bring Your Own Mac

────────── C

C&G	Chuckle and Grin
CADET	Can't Add, Doesn't Even Try
CID	Crying In Disgrace
CMIIW	Correct Me If Im Wrong
CO	(1) Conference. (2) Company
CSG	Chuckle, Snicker, Grin
CU	See You
CU2	See You, Too
CUL	See You Later
CUL8R	See You Later
CULA	See You Later, Alligator
CWYL	Chat With You Later
CYA	(1) See Ya. (2) Cover Your Ass
CYAL8R	See You All Later

D

DIIK	Damned If I Know
DIKU?	Do I Know You?
DIY	Do It Yourself
DK	Don't Know
DLTBBB	Don't Let The Bed Bugs Bite
dotgov	A government official
DTRT	Do The Right Thing
DWIMC	Do What I Mean, Correctly
DWIMNWIS	Do What I Mean, Not What I Say

E

ESAD	Eat Shit And Die
ETLA	Extended Three Letter Acronym

F

F2F	Face To Face
FCFS	First Come, First Served
FISH	First In, Still Here
FITB	Fill In The Blank
FOAD	Fuck Off And Die
FOAF	Friend Of A Friend
FS	For Sale
FTASB	Faster Than A Speeding Bullet
FTF	Face to Face

FTL	Faster Than Light
FUBAR	Fouled Up Beyond All Repair
FUBB	Fouled Up Beyond Belief
FUD	Fear, Uncertainty and Doubt
FURTB	Full Up Ready To Burst
FWIW	For What It's Worth
FYA	For Your Amusement
FYI	For Your Information

——————— G

GA	Go Ahead
GAL	Get A Life
GD&R	Grinning, Ducking and Running
GD&RF	Grinning, Ducking, and Running Fast
GD&WVVF	Grinning, Ducking, and Walking Very, Very Fast
GDW	Grin, Duck and Weave
GF	Girl Friend
GFN	Gone For Now
GFR	Grim File Reaper
GIWIST	Gee, I Wish I'd Said That
GLGH	Good Luck and Good Hunting
GMTA	Great Minds Think Alike
GOWI	Get On With It
GTSY	Great To See You

H

H&K	Hugs and Kisses
HAK	Hugs And Kisses
HHIS	Hanging Head In Shame
HHO	1/2 K Ha, Ha, Only Half Kidding
HHOJ	Ha Ha Only Joking
HHOK	Ha Ha Only Kidding
HHOS	Ha Ha Only Serious
HHTYAY	Happy Holidays To You And Yours
HOYEW	Hanging On Your Every Word
HSIK	How Should I Know
HTH	Hope That Helps!

I

IAAA	I Am An Accountant
IAAL	I Am A Lawyer
IAE	In Any Event
IANAA	I Am Not An Accountant
IANAL	I Am Not A Lawyer
IAW	In Accordance With
IBTD	I Beg To Differ
IC	I See
IIABDFI	If It Ain't Broke, Don't Fix It
IIRC	If I Remember Correctly
IIWM	If It Were Me ... (or) If It Were Mine ...

IJWTK	I Just Want To Know
IJWTS	I Just Want To Say
IKWUM	I Know What You Mean
IMA	I Might Add
IMAO	In My Arrogant Opinion
IMCO	In My Considered Opinion
IME	In My Experience
IMHO	In My Humble Opinion
IMNSHO	In My Not So Humble Opinion
IMO	In My Opinion
IMPOV	In My Point Of View
INPO	In No Particular Order
IOW	In Other Words
IRL	(1) In Real Life (chat). (2) Industrial Robot Language
ISS	I'm So Sure
ISSYGTI	I'm So Sure You Get The Idea!
ISWIM	If (you) See What I Mean
ITFA	In The Final Analysis
ITSFWI	If The Shoe Fits, Wear It
IWALU	I Will Always Love You
IWBNI	It Would Be Nice If
IYFEG	Insert Your Favorite Ethnic Group (for ethnic jokes)
IYSWIM	If You See What I Mean

J

JAM	Just A Minute
JAS	Just A Second
JIC	Just In Case
JMO	Just My Opinion
JSNM	Just Stark Naked Magic
JTLYK	Just To Let You Know

K

k	Okay
KHYF	Know How You Feel
KIBO	Knowledge In, Bullshit Out
KISS	Keep It Simple, Stupid
KIT	Keep In Touch
KMA	Kiss My Ass
KWIM	Know What I Mean?
KYFC	Keep Your Fingers Crossed

L

L	Laugh
L8R	Later
LABATYD	Life's A Bitch And Then You Die
LJBF	Lets Just Be Friends
LLTA	Lots and Lots of Thundering Applause
LMAO	Laughing My Ass Off
LMHO	Laughing My Head Off

LOL	....	Laughing Out Loud
LSHMBA	....	Laughing So Hard My Belly Aches
LSHMBH	....	Laughing So Hard My Belly Hurts
LTHTT	....	Laughing Too Hard To Type
LTNS	....	Long Time, No See
LTNT	....	Long Time, No Type
LTS	....	Laughing To Self
LUWAMH	....	Love You With All My Heart
LY	....	Love You

———— M

MLA	....	Multiple Letter Acronym
MOF	....	Matter Of Fact
MOTAS	....	Member Of The Appropriate Sex
MOTD	....	Message Of The Day
MOTOS	....	Member Of The Opposite Sex
MOTSS	....	Member Of The Same Sex
MTF	....	More To Follow
MTFBWY	....	May The Force Be With You
MYOB	....	Mind Your Own Business

———— N

NAVY	....	Never Again Volunteer Yourself
NBD	....	No Big Deal
NFW	....	No Fucking Way!
NHOH	....	Never Heard Of Him/Her

NIH	....	Not Invented Here
NIMBY	....	Not In My Back Yard
NINO	....	No Input, No Output
NOYB	....	None Of Your Business
NP	....	No Problem
NQA	....	No Questions Asked
NTIM	....	Not That It Matters
NTIMM	....	Not That It Matters Much
NTW	....	Not To Worry
NTYMI	....	Now That You Mention It

———————— O

O	....	Over
OATUS	....	On A Totally Unrelated Subject
OAUS	....	On An Unrelated Subject
OBO	....	Or Best Offer
OBTW	....	Oh, By The Way
OIC	....	Oh, I See
ONNA	....	Oh No, Not Again
ONNTA	....	Oh No, Not This Again
OO	....	Over and Out
OOTC	....	Obligatory On-Topic Comment
OTFL	....	On the Floor Laughing
OTL	....	Out To Lunch
OTOH	....	On The Other Hand

OTOOH	On The Other Other Hand
OTT	Over The Top
OTTH	On The Third Hand
OTTOMH	Off The Top Of My Head
OWTTE	Or Words To That Effect

——————— P

PABG	Packing A Big Gun
PDS	Please Don't Shout
PLOKTA	Press Lots Of Keys To Abort
PMBI	Pardon My Butting In
PMF	Pardon My French
PMFBI	Pardon Me For Butting In
PMFJI	Pardon Me For Jumping In
PMIGBOM	Put Mind In Gear, Before Opening Mouth
PMJI	Pardon My Jumping In
PNCAH	Please, No Cursing Allowed Here
POSSLQ	Person Of Opposite Sex Sharing Living Quarters
PPL	People
PTMM	Please Tell Me More

——————— R

R U THERE?	Are you there?
RAEBNC	Read And Enjoyed, But No Comment
re	(1) Hello again. (2) In regard to
rehi	Hi again

RHIP	Rank Has Its Privileges
RL	Real Life
RLCO	Real Life Conference
ROFL	Rolling On Floor Laughing
ROFLASTC	Rolling On Floor Laughing And Scaring The Cat
ROFLGO	Rolling On Floor Laughing Guts Out
ROFLMAO	Rolling On Floor Laughing My Arse Off
ROTF	Rolling On The Floor
ROTFL	Rolling On The Floor Laughing
ROTFLOL	Rolling On The Floor Laughing Out Loud
RRQ	Return Receipt Request
RSN	Real Soon Now
RSVP	Respondez S'il Vous Plaît, i.e. 'please reply'
RTBM	Read The Bloody Manual
RTFAQ	Read The Frequently Asked Questions
RTFF	Read The Fucking FAQ
RTFM	Read The Fucking Manual
RTM	Read The Manual
RTSM	Read The Silly Manual
RTWFQ	Read The Whole Fucking Question
RYFM	Read Your Friendly Manual
RYS	Read Your Screen

———— S

S	Smile

SAPFU	Surpassing All Previous Foul Ups
SCNR	Sorry, Could Not Resist
SEC	Wait a second
SETE	Smiling Ear To Ear
SFLA	Stupid Four Letter Acronym
SICS	Sitting In Chair Snickering
SLM	See Last Mail
SMOP	Small Matter Of Programming
SNAFU	Situation Normal: All Fouled Up
SO	Significant Other
SOL	Shit Out Of Luck
SOS	(1) Same Old Stuff. (2) Help!
SOW	Speaking Of Which
SUFID	Screwing Up Face In Disgust
SWIM	See What I Mean?
SWL	Screaming With Laughter
SYS	See You Soon

———————— T

TAF	That's All, Folks!
TAFN	That's All For Now
TANJ	There Ain't No Justice
TANSTAAFL	There Ain't No Such Thing As A Free Lunch
TARFU	Things Are Really Fouled Up
TBYB	Try Before You Buy

TDM .... Too Darn Many

TFS .... Three Finger Salute (Ctl-Alt-Del)

TFTHAOT .... Thanx For The Help Ahead Of Time

TFTT .... Thanks For The Thought

TGAL .... Think Globally, Act Locally

THX .... Thanks

TIA .... Thanks In Advance

TIC .... Tongue In Cheek

TINWIS .... That Is Not What I Said

TNSTAAFL .... There's No Such Thing As A Free Lunch

TNTL .... Trying Not To Laugh

TNX .... Thanks

TNXE6 .... Thanks A Million

TOBAL .... There Oughta Be A Law

TOBG .... This Oughta Be Good

TOY .... Thinking Of You

TPTB .... The Powers That Be

TRDMC .... Tears Running Down My Cheeks

TSR .... Totally Stupid Rules

TTBOMK .... To The Best Of My Knowledge

TTFN .... Ta Ta For Now

TTKSF .... Trying To Keep a Straight Face

TTUL .... Talk To You Later

TTYAWFN .... Talk To You A While From Now

TTYL .... Talk To You Later

TTYT	....	Talk To You Tomorrow
TYCLO	....	Turn Your CAPS LOCK Off (Stop shouting)
TYVM	....	Thank You Very Much

─────── U

UOK	....	Are You OK?

─────── W

WAEF	....	When All Else Fails
WB	....	Welcome Back
WDYMBT	....	What Do You Mean By That?
WDYT	....	What Do You Think?
WIBAMU	....	Well, I'll Be A Monkey's Uncle
WIBNI	....	Wouldn't It Be Nice If
WMMOWS	....	Wash My Mouth Out With Soap
WNOHGB	....	Where No One Has Gone Before
WOA	....	Work Of Art
WOTAM	....	Waste Of Time And Money
WRT	....	With Regard To, or With Respect To
WT	....	Without Thinking
WTB	....	Want To Buy
WTF	....	What The Fuck?
WTG	....	Way To Go!
WTGP	....	Want To Go Private?
WTH	....	What The Hell?
WTTM	....	Without Thinking Too Much

WYGISWYPF .... What You Get Is What You Pay For

——————— X

XOXOXO .... Kisses and hugs

——————— Y

YABA .... Yet Another Bloody Acronym

YAOTM .... Yet Another Off-Topic Message

YAUN .... Yet Another Unix Nerd

YGLT .... You're Gonna Love This ...

YGTI .... You Get The Idea?

YGWYPF .... You Get What You Pay For

YIU .... Yes, I Understand

YIWGP .... Yes, I Will Go Private

YKYARW .... You Know You're A Redneck When ...

YMMV .... Your Mileage May Vary

——————— MISC

! .... 'have a comment'

$0.02 .... Throwing in your two cents' worth

<arching eyebrows> .... Speaker arches eyebrows

<chuckle> .... Speaker chuckles

<frown> .... Speaker is frowning

<g> .... Grin

<grin> .... Speaker is grinning

<smile> .... The one writing the message is smiling

<smirk> .... The one writing the message is smirking

<wink> .... The one writing the message is winking

501 .... An excuse that's full of holes

? .... 'have a question'

Acknowledgements

- SpeedyGrl.com
  http://www.speedygrl.com/osquotes.html

- SoftwareQuotes.com

- WorldofQuotes.com

- Wikipedia.org

- quotesplace.com

- MotivationalQuotes.Com
  http://www.motivationalquotes.com

- Computer quotes
  http://www.gdargaud.net/Humor/
  QuotesComputer.html

- Question.com

- ThinkExist.com

- The Quotations Page
  http://www.quotationspage.com

- comedy-zone-net
  http://www.comedy-zone.net/quotes/
  Science_and_Technology/computers.htm

- Famous Computer (mostly) Quotes
  http://ifaq.wap.org/computers/famousquotes.html

- www.sysprog.net/

- QuotesWeb.com

- The Quote Garden
  http://www.quotegarden.com

- *zaadz
  http://www.zaadz.com

- Faisal N. Jawdat
  http://www.faisal.com/quotes/s.html

- GIGA Quotes
  http://www.giga-usa.com

Fair Use Statement

From 'Copyright Law of the United States of America and Related Laws Contained in Title 17 of the United States Code'

§ 107. Limitations on exclusive rights: Fair use

Notwithstanding the provisions of sections 106 and 106A, the fair use of a copyrighted work, including such use by reproduction in copies or phonorecords or by any other means specified by that section, for purposes such as criticism, comment, news reporting, teaching (including multiple copies for classroom use), scholarship, or research, is not an infringement of copyright.

VINCENT F. HENDRICKS

⊢ 1970—

Vincent F. Hendricks holds two doctoral degrees in philosophy (dr. phil. and PhD) and is Professor of Epistemology, Logic and Methodology. His professional interests focus on the intersection between formal and mainstream philosophy—especially as it relates to epistemology, logic and philosophy of science.

Vincent F. Hendricks is the author and/or editor of numerous books and articles on epistemology, methodology and logic. Among his most recent books are *The Convergence of Scientific Knowledge—a View from the Limit* (Kluwer 2001), *Modern Elementary Logic* (Høst & Søn 2002) and *Mainstream and Formal Epistemology* (Cambridge University Press 2005).

In 2002 Vincent F. Hendricks founded ΦLOG—The Network for Philosophical Logic and Its Applications, and started the associated ΦNEWS—The Newsletter for Philosophical Logic and its Applications published by Springer.

He is editor-in-chief of *Synthese* and *Synthese Library*, the highly esteemed journal and book series in philosophy published by Springer.

In 2005 Vincent F. Hendricks founded

$$\frac{\text{VINCE}}{\text{INC}}\text{.com}$$

a platform for promoting philosophy to a layman audience. As parts of this endeavor are the collections of pertinent, critical and humorous citations and aphorisms about philosophy and its broader intellectual environment, in particular the trilogy

FEISTY FRAGMENTS: FOR PHILOSOPHY

LOGICAL LYRICS: FROM PHILOSOPHY TO POETICS

500 CC: Computer Citations

published by King's College Publications, London.

THE TRILOGY

FEISTY FRAGMENTS: FOR PHILOSOPHY

⊢ September 2004

Feisty Fragments: For Philosophy is a collection of more than 550 quotations from people from all walks of life expressing their rather critical and often quite humorous takes on both philosophy and philosophers—from Nietzsche to Einstein, from Catherine the Great to John F. Kennedy.

> It is a wonderful collection with a fine presentation. We're all enjoying everything from Quine (of course) and Queen Victoria to Charlie Brown. —Douglas B. Quine

LOGICAL LYRICS: FROM PHILOSOPHY TO POETICS

⊢ March 2005

Logical Lyrics: From Philosophy to Poetics is a collection of citations and aphorisms from all sorts of people – from Napoleon Bonaparte to Human League – expressing their embracing, critical and humorous views on logic and logical matters.

> I found this collection utterly absorbing from beginning to end. It combines some very sagacious ideas with some choice bits that are delightfully funny. —Raymond M. Smullyan

500 CC: Computer Citations

⊢ September 2005

'hAS aNYONE sEEN MY cAPSLOCK kEY?' *500 CC* records the experiences we have as computer users, abusers and Internet-cruisers—from rage and anger via joy, laughter and appreciation to despair and frustration.

> 500CC contains an amazing assortment of computer related quotes. It's the sort of book you put down and then simply must pick up again 5 minutes later. If you only ever buy two books about Computing, then buy this one twice and give one copy to a friend. —Kevin Warwick

Index

breakfast, 80
brickmaker, 114
broadcasting, 25
buffer, 11, 22
bug, 8, 73
buggery, 6
bugs, 4, 82
Bunny, 82
Bush, 65
business, 32, 44

cabbage, 126
caffeine, 125
calculator, 11
Caligula, 50
cAPSLOCK, 17
car, 59, 80
car accidents, 10
carbon paper, 18
castles, 28
cathedral, 12
cats, 9, 96
caviar, 128
CD, 4
censorship, 53
cereal, 80
chain saw, 56
cheerleaders, 78
cheese-grater, 40
Cheetos, 115
chess, 76
chicken entrails, 111
children, 17, 35, 39, 119
chilluns, 4
chimpanzee, 113
chip, 34
civilization, 127
cliches, 95
cloning, 118
cocaine, 113

cocktail waitress, 135
code, 6, 12–14, 19, 31, 55, 73, 107, 118, 127
source, 10
coder, 119
coffee, 40, 115
cognitive elite, 46
cognoscenti, 43
Coke, 121
COMMAND.COM, 3
committee, 26
committees, 8, 80
commode, 4
common culture, 39
commonsense, 111
communication, 11
compact disc, 81
compassion, 52
compiler, 15, 16, 63
complexity, 41, 73, 76, 128
compress, 4
computer, 4, 15, 37, 40, 41, 43, 82, 86
home, 61
Mac, 6
mainframe, 18
NeXT, 18
PalmPilot, 96
PC, 6, 10, 18, 71, 83, 91
PDA, 91
PowerPC, 119
von Neuman, 21
computer afficionados, 115
computer bums, 128
computer crash, 4
computer geek, 40
computer manuals, 33
computer poetry, 118
computer problems, 14

Venus, 9
version, 25
virgin, 61
virus, 3, 4, 20, 35
virus scan, 8

water, 14
waterfall, 55
weapons, 103
web, 4, 16
websites, 103
whale, 68
wheel chair, 8
white noise, 11
wife, 12
windows, 3
WipeMe 1.0, 96
wire cutters, 135
wisdom, 47
wizards, 9
women, 17
wood pulp, 40
woodpecker, 127
World Wide Web, 115
writing, 47

Y1K, 15
Year 2000 compliant, 17